C000097029

Lease or L

The law after
Street v *Mountford*

Kim Lewison
MA, Barrister

Longman Professional

©Longman Group Ltd 1985

Published by

Longman Professional and Business Communications Division
Longman Group Limited
21-27 Lamb's Conduit Street, London WC1N 3NJ

ISBN 0-85121-124-0

Associated Offices

Australia	Longman Professional Publishing (Pty) Limited
	130 Phillip Street, Sydney, NSW 2000
Hong Kong	Longman Group (Far East) Limited
	Cornwall House, 18th Floor, Taikoo Trading Estate,
	Tong Chong Street, Quarry Bay
Malaysia	Longman Malaysia Sdn Bhd
	Wisma Damansara/Tingkat 2, 5 Jalan Semantan,
	Peti Surat 63, Kuala Lumpur 01-02
Singapore	Longman Singapore Publishers (Pte) Ltd
	25 First Lok Yang Road, Singapore 2262
USA	Longman Group (USA) Inc
	500 North Dearborn Street, Chicago, Illinois 60610

Printed and bound in Great Britain by
Biddles Ltd, Guildford and King's Lynn

Contents

Appendix

Preface

On 2 May 1985 the House of Lords delivered judgment in *Street v Mountford*. The leading speech was given by Lord Templeman with whom the other Lords of Appeal (Lords Scarman, Keith of Kinkel, Bridge of Harwich and Brightman) agreed. The case is reported at (1985) 274 EG 821; [1985] 2 WLR 877; [1985] 2 All ER 289. It has disapproved a line of cases decided in the Court of Appeal since the war (the leading judgments being given mainly by Denning LJ and, as he became, Lord Denning MR), and has reaffirmed the importance of exclusive possession as the distinction between a lease and a licence. This monograph seeks to analyse the effect of the case on property transactions, both residential and commercial. I have tried to state the law as at 1 June 1985.

Kim Lewison
Temple EC4

Table of Cases

1 Where Did the Law Go Wrong?

1.1 The traditional view

The traditional view of the nature of a licence was expressed more than 300 years ago by Vaughan CJ as follows:

A dispensation or licence properly passeth no interest nor alters or transfers property in any thing, but only makes an action lawful, which without it had been unlawful (*Thomas* v *Sorrell* (1673) Vaughan 351).

Viewed in this way a person who has only a licence has none of the property rights of an owner of land, even a limited owner. He cannot, for example, exclude strangers from the land, still less the grantor of the licence. So it came about that the law regarded the grant of a right of exclusive possession as the hallmark of a tenancy. The apogee of this approach is to be found in *Lynes* v *Snaith* [1899] 1 QB 487. In April 1884 John Snaith gave his daughter-in-law permission to live rent free in a cottage which he owned. She entered into possession. Thirteen years later John Snaith died and his personal representatives sued for possession. On appeal from the county court, the Divisional Court held that the daughter-in-law had been a tenant at will, who had acquired title by adverse possession. Lawrence J said:

I think it is clear that she was a tenant at will and not a licensee; for the admissions state that she was in exclusive possession—a fact which is wholly inconsistent with her having been a mere licensee.

Seventy-five years later, on indistinguishable facts, the court reached the opposite conclusion (*Heslop* v *Burns* [1974] 3 All ER 406). This radical change in the approach of the courts is a product of a series of cases in the Court of Appeal decided since the war. Denning LJ (or Lord Denning MR as he became) sat in nearly all of them.

1.2   The starting point: intention of the parties

The start of the new approach is the judgment of Denning LJ in *Errington* v *Errington and Woods* [1952] 1 KB 290. Mr Errington bought a house in Newcastle with the aid of a mortgage as a home for his son who had recently married Mary Errington, the first defendant. The father handed Mary Errington the building society's pass book and told her that the house would be hers and her husband's when they had paid the last instalment on the mortgage. The house remained in the father's name, and when he died his widow sued for possession. The county court judge held that the son and daughter-in-law were tenants at will. The Court of Appeal disagreed. Denning LJ (with whom Somervell LJ agreed) referred to the traditional view that in distinguishing between a licence and a tenancy 'a crucial test has sometimes been supposed to be whether the occupier has exclusive possession or not'. He then referred to a number of cases, and concluded:

The result of all these cases is that, although a person who is let into exclusive possession is prima facie to be considered to be a tenant, nevertheless he will not be held to be so if the circumstances negative any intention to create a tenancy. Words alone may not suffice. Parties cannot turn a tenancy into a licence merely by calling it one. But if the circumstances and the conduct of the parties show that all was intended was that the occupier should be granted a personal privilege, with no interest in the land, he will be held to be a licensee only. In view of these recent cases I doubt whether *Lynes* v *Snaith* and the case of the gamekeeper referred to therein, would be decided the same way today.

This formulation of the law removes the emphasis from the grant of exclusive possession and transfers it to the intention of the parties. The court's true task is to discover what was intended. The cases referred to by Denning LJ all fell into special categories, eg where the parties did not intend to enter into legal relations at all; or where the grantor had no legal power to grant a tenancy; or where the relationship was that of master and service occupier or of vendor and purchaser. Accordingly, to the extent that the passage quoted above leaves the question of intention at large, it was not supported by the authorities cited, and marked a new departure.

1.3 The next step

Cobb v *Lane* [1952] 1 All ER 1199 marks the next step. Miss Lane bought a house for her brother to live in. He lived there with his wife and family, with the possession which people normally have in their homes. On the death of Miss Lane, her executors sued for possession. The county court judge found that there was never any intention on the part of any of the parties concerned of creating any legal relationship. His decision was upheld on appeal. Denning LJ said:

The question in all these cases is one of intention: did the circumstances and the conduct of the parties show that all that was intended was that the occupier should have a personal privilege with no interest in the land?

This formulation emphasises more strongly the intention of the parties, and by putting the 'circumstances and the conduct of the parties' in second place relegates those features to evidential status only. Moreover, there is no mention of exclusive possession.

This approach was applied by McNair J in *Murray Bull & Co Ltd* v *Murray* [1953] 1 QB 211. Mr Murray was the managing director of the plaintiff company. He occupied a flat on the company's premises under a tenancy for seven years determinable on the termination of his directorship. At the expiry of the term he continued in possession. Later he resigned his directorship and asked the company whether he could stay on until he found other accommodation. The company agreed. On those facts he was held to be a licensee. McNair J said:

In the circumstances of the present case, and on the proper construction of the documents ... I think it is plain ... that both parties intended that the relationship should be that of licensee and no more, though they may not have used that precise term or even had that precise term in mind. The primary consideration on both sides was that the defendant, as occupant of that flat should not be a controlled tenant. I think it is clear that their common intention was that the defendant as the occupier should, to use the language of

Denning LJ, be granted a mere personal privilege with no interest in the premises.

The judge did not think it necessary to consider whether Mr Murray had exclusive possession, but proceeded straight to an evaluation of the intention of the parties with aid of such of the evidence as he thought of assistance.

1.4   The new test: is the agreement 'personal'?

Having discarded the test of exclusive possession as the distinguishing feature between a licence and a tenancy, it clearly became necessary to formulate some different test to determine which of the two was intended by the parties. The new test, selected primarily by Lord Denning MR on his return to the Court of Appeal from the House of Lords, was whether the agreement was personal or not. The test first appeared in *Abbeyfield (Harpenden) Society Ltd* v *Woods* [1968] 1 All ER 352. The defendant was the sole occupier of a room in an old people's home. There was no written agreement, but the plaintiff company had written the defendant a letter in which it was stated that the company reserved the right to take possession of his room should it think fit, but promised to give one month's notice before doing so. Lord Denning MR said:

> The modern cases show that a man may be a licensee even though he has exclusive possession, even though the word 'rent' is used and even though the word 'tenancy' is used. The court must look at the agreement as a whole and see whether a tenancy really was intended. In this case there is, besides the one room, the provision of services, meals, a resident housekeeper, and such like. The whole arrangement was so personal in nature that the proper inference is . . . that he was a licensee on the terms stated in the letter.

This test does not require the court to pay any attention to the question of exclusive possession or to the language used by the parties. It concentrates on whether the 'arrangement' is personal or not. This approach was repeated by Lord Denning MR in *Shell-Mex and BP Ltd* v *Manchester Garages Ltd* [1971] 1 All ER 841:

> Broadly speaking, we have to see whether it is a personal privilege given to a person, in which case it is a licence, or whether it grants an

interest in land, in which case it is a tenancy. At one time it used to be thought that exclusive possession was a decisive factor, but that is not so. It depends on broader considerations altogether. Primarily on whether it is personal in its nature or not: see *Errington* v *Errington and Woods*.

The reference to *Errington*'s case is misleading because, as has been seen the test adumbrated there was based upon circumstances and the conduct of the parties negativing a prima facie inference that a person with exclusive possession was a tenant. The prime consideration is now stated to be whether the arrangement is personal or not. What was once a consequence of a finding that a licence existed had been transformed into a determining factor in establishing the existence itself.

Lord Denning's final word on the distinction between licence and tenancy was spoken in *Marchant* v *Charters* [1977] 3 All ER 918. Mrs Marchant owned a house divided into seven bed-sitting rooms. She described it as a self-catering residential hotel for single men. Each room was furnished, and cleaned daily. Clean linen was provided weekly. Meals were available by arrangement with the housekeeper. Mr Charters, the occupier of one of the rooms, was held to be a licensee. Lord Denning MR said:

Gathering the cases together, what does it come to? What is the test to see whether the occupier of one room in a house is a tenant or a licensee? It does not depend on whether he or she has exclusive possession or not. It does not depend on whether the room is furnished or not. It does not depend on whether the occupation is permanent or temporary. It does not depend on the label which the parties put on it. All these are factors which may influence the decision but none of them is conclusive. All the circumstances have to be worked out. Eventually the answer depends on the nature and quality of the occupancy. Was it intended that the occupier should have a stake in the room or did he have only permission for himself personally to occupy the room, whether under a contract or not, in which case he is a licensee?

Although it was not difficult to identify a case where an occupier only had personal permission to occupy a room in a house, it was extremely difficult to identify a case where an occupier was intended to have a 'stake' in the room. Partly this was because of the difficulty in understanding what a 'stake' was. The way in which Lord Denning put the test left the possibility that a permanent occupier of an unfurnished room with exclusive possession of it might be held to be a licensee, but in what circumstances this might be so was not clear. What was clear, however, was that the test had moved a long way since *Lynes* v *Snaith*.

1.5   A parallel line: construing the written agreement

In the main, the cases referred to above did not involve the construction of written agreements. The normal task of the court in construing a written agreement is to ascertain the true intention of the parties, as revealed by the words they used. By contrast, where there is no written agreement the court often treats the discovery of the relationship between the parties as a matter of pure fact (*Torbett* v *Faulkner* [1952] 2 TLR 659 per Romer LJ). The process of construction would seem to accord with the test of intention gathered from all the circumstances. In parallel with the cases which did not involve written agreements, the Court of Appeal was evolving a body of law concerning the construction of written agreements to see whether they gave rise to licences or tenancies.

1.6   An early example: *Taylor* v *Caldwell*

In *Taylor* v *Caldwell* (1863) 3 B & S 826 Mr Taylor and another agreed to take and Mr Caldwell and another agreed to let the Surrey Gardens and Music Hall on four specified days for the purpose of giving a series of four grand concerts. The rent was £100 for each day. Mr Caldwell was to provide an organised military and quadrille band, al fresco entertainments of various descriptions; coloured minstrels; fireworks; a ballet; a wizard; tight rope performances; rifle galleries; air gun shooting; boats on the lake and aquatic sports and Chinese and Persian games. It was held that despite the use of language appropriate to a lease, exclusive possession had not been given to Mr Taylor, and consequently no demise had been created. Given the variety of entertainment which the 'landlord' had to provide, this hardly seems surprising.

1.7 The modern cases

The first of the modern cases is *Facchini* v *Bryson* [1952] 1 TLR 1386. Mr Facchini employed Mr Bryson in his ice-cream business as an assistant. He permitted Mr Bryson to occupy a house on the terms of a written agreement in consideration of a weekly payment. The agreement contained a stipulation requiring the occupier to allow the owner to enter the house to examine its condition, and a stipulation prohibiting assignment, underletting and parting with possession. The agreement also provided that 'nothing in this agreement shall be construed to create a tenancy'. The Court of Appeal held that despite that provision the agreement did create a tenancy. Somervell LJ held that the obligations undertaken by the occupier were consistent only with a tenancy, especially the prohibition on underletting, and that the parties could not alter that conclusion merely by a deeming provision. Denning LJ agreed but put his decision on a broader base:

In all the cases where an occupier has been held to be a licensee there has been something in the circumstances, such as a family arrangement, an act of friendship or generosity, or such like, to negative any intention to create a tenancy. . . . In the present case, however, there are no special circumstances. It is a simple case where the employer let a man into occupation of a house in consequence of his employment at a weekly sum payable by him. The occupation has all the features of a service tenancy, and the parties cannot by the mere words of their contract turn it into something else.

The broad expression of principle was not strictly necessary to the decision in the case, but it has been much cited, even if less frequently applied.

The approach of Somervell LJ was taken up by the Court of Appeal in *Addiscombe Garden Estates Ltd* v *Crabbe* [1958] 1 QB 513. The defendants were the trustees of a tennis club which occupied a club house and tennis courts in the grounds of a hotel upon the terms of a written agreement. The approach of the court was stated by Jenkins LJ as follows:

It does not necessarily follow that a document described as a licence is, merely on that account, to be regarded as amounting only to a licence in law. The whole of the document must be looked at; and if after it has been examined, the right conclusion appears to be that, whatever label may have been attached to it, it in fact conferred and imposed on the grantee in substance the rights and obligations of a tenant, and on the grantor the rights and obligations of a landlord, then it must be given the appropriate effect, that is to say, it must be treated as a tenancy agreement as distinct from a mere licence.

This approach does not treat the label given to the document by the parties as worthless; it merely prevents it from being conclusive. Whether a document creates a licence or a tenancy is to be gathered from construing the agreement as a whole, including what the parties chose to call it. The court proceeded to construe the written agreement, and concluded that it created a tenancy. The particular features of the agreement which led the court to that conclusion were:

  (i) the authority given to the trustees to 'enter upon use and enjoy' the property;
 (ii) the grant of a term certain;
(iii) the payment of a money sum in advance at regular intervals;
 (iv) the occupier's obligation to keep the club house in repair;
  (v) a prohibition on cutting down plants and removing soil and clay;
 (vi) an obligation to permit the owner to inspect the condition of the property;
(vii) the occupier's obligation to insure;
(viii) a covenant for quiet enjoyment; and
 (ix) a proviso for re-entry.

In effect the agreement contained all the features of a lease of commercial property, save that the terminology was that of licensor and licensee. This case, therefore, is a case which turned on the construction of a particular document.

1.8   The sharing cases

In the second half of the last decade there emerged the sharing agreement. Such an agreement permitted the sharer to share residential accommodation either with the landlord or with nominees of the landlord. In practice the sharers often signed agreements as a group, and sometimes were living together as one household or as man and wife. The principle behind the sharing agreement was to prevent an occupier of residential property not only from having a tenancy of it but also from having exclusive occupation of any part of it which might attract the protection available to the holder of a restricted contract (see Rent Act 1977, s 19).

The first of these cases to come before the Court of Appeal was *Somma* v *Hazlehurst* [1978] 2 All ER 1011. H and S, an unmarried couple, simultaneously signed agreements permitting each of them to share with the other. The issue in the case was whether the two agreements should be construed as one single agreement or as a composite agreement conferring exclusive possession on H and S jointly. The Court of Appeal held that to construe the two agreements as conferring a joint interest on H and S would not be construing the agreements, but rewriting them in the absence of an allegation of fraud or a claim for rectification. However, the court proceeded to construe the agreements together (on the assumption that they should have been read together) to see whether the terms of the agreements prevented the joint occupation from being exclusive. After a detailed examination of the terms of the agreements the court came to the conclusion that even if read together the agreements did not confer a right either of exclusive possession or exclusive occupation of the property. It was not argued that the agreements were shams.

The Court of Appeal followed a similar line of approach in *Aldrington Garages Ltd* v *Fielder* (1978) 37 P & CR 461. A man and a woman simultaneously signed agreements permitting them to share a flat. They went into occupation. Subsequently the woman left, and the man continued in occupation paying the amount specified in his agreement (which was half the aggregate amount payable by both occupiers). The owners of the property sued for possession. The Court of Appeal held that they were entitled to succeed. Geoffrey Lane LJ treated the important question as being whether, on the true construction of the agreements, exclusive possession had or had not been granted to the occupiers (see p 469). His overall approach was summarised as follows:

If what the parties have agreed is truly a licence and not a tenancy dressed up in the verbiage or trappings or clothing of a licence then the owner is entitled to succeed. It is not a situation, if there is such a situation, in which the court should allow itself to be influenced one way or the other by sympathy.

As in *Somma* v *Hazlehurst* the court held that to treat the two agreements as giving rise to a single composite right would have been to rewrite rather than to construe the agreements. The particular sticking point was the division of responsibility for payment, because the court held that if the interest had been a joint interest then both occupiers would have been liable for the whole of the moneys payable for the flat rather than half each.

In two cases, however, the court reached a different conclusion on the facts. In *Demuren* v *Seal Estates Ltd* (1978) 249 EG 440 the Court of Appeal held that the two sharing agreements signed by two students were shams which did not reflect the real bargain between the parties. However, Megaw LJ would have been prepared to hold that in exceptional circumstances a joint tenancy could be created under which each joint tenant was only liable for payment of one half of the rent. In the second case, *O'Malley* v *Seymour* (1978) 250 EG 108, a sharing arrangement was again held on the facts not to reflect the real agreement between the parties and the court held that a tenancy had been created.

The last of the sharing cases was *Sturolson & Co* v *Weniz* (1984) 272 EG 326. Mr Weniz, his wife and a friend wanted to share a flat together. They found a flat and each signed sharing agreements on the same day in identical terms. It was conceded that as a matter of construction each agreement was a licence rather than a tenancy. However, it was argued on behalf of Mr Weniz that the agreements were shams. The Court of Appeal rejected that argument. Eveleigh LJ said that all parties knew what they were doing, and Mr Weniz realised that the landlord would not have let him have the flat unless he signed an agreement to which the Rent Act 1977 did not apply. In consequence it could not be said that the agreements were shams, since they achieved the objective which both parties intended them to achieve. Fox LJ agreed, saying:

In my view, both parties certainly intended to execute this agreement and they understood its terms. It may be that the agreement was the only way in which the defendant could get into the premises, but that is not a reason for saying that the parties' true intention was different from what it appears to be on the face of the document.

Thus by the time of the decision of the Court of Appeal in *Sturolson & Co* v *Weniz* it was well established that by a carefully drafted agreement whose effect was clearly understood by all parties a property owner could effectively contract out of the Rent Act. It should be noted that all the cases which came before the court involving sharing agreements were cases in which the sharers were known to each other (and in some cases living together) before moving in to the property in question. Whether it would have made any difference to those cases where the owner lost if the sharers had been strangers to each other will be considered hereafter.

1.9   The climax

The climax of the tendency to conjure a licence out of an arm's length grant of exclusive possession came in the decision of the Court of Appeal in *Eastleigh BC* v *Walsh* (19 November 1984, unreported). Mr Walsh was homeless. The local authority offered him accommodation. He was given the keys of a council house and a document headed 'conditions of tenancy'. The conditions of tenancy were all consistent only with the grant of a tenancy. The Court of Appeal held that Mr Walsh had been granted a licence. Griffiths LJ said:

In my view this judge was entitled . . . to conclude as he did, that a council giving emergency shelter . . . was not intending to create a tenancy despite the fact that they foolishly used the same paperwork as they used for their ordinary council tenants, and that he was further entitled to draw the inference that the occupant well realised that that was the true state of affairs.

The court had travelled a long way since *Lynes* v *Snaith*. Not only was the fact of exclusive possession overridden, but so also was the fact that the parties had entered into a written agreement described as a tenancy, and containing obligations appropriate to and consistent with the grant of a tenancy. Nor was there any element of charity or friendship between the parties, since the local authority was acting in fulfilment of a statutory duty imposed upon it by the Housing (Homeless Persons) Act 1977.

The time was ripe for a review of the law by the House of Lords.

2 The Law Corrected

2.1 Construing the written agreement

It has already been seen that in *Eastleigh BC* v *Walsh* the Court of Appeal relegated the written agreement to the category of mere 'paperwork'. The House of Lords unanimously rejected this approach (see [1985] 2 All ER 112). Lord Bridge of Harwich, who delivered the only speech said:

> The appellant was granted exclusive possession of the house on terms which are fully set out in the contemporaneous documents, viz the local authority's offer of a tenancy . . . the appellant's acceptance of that offer . . . and the document entitled 'Conditions of Tenancy' . . . . Reading these unambiguous documents in the light of the express statutory provision in Sch 3, para 5 of the 1980 Act that a tenancy granted in pursuance of section 3(4) of the 1977 Act . . . is not a secure tenancy I can see no ground for any finding that the 'nature of the occupancy' of the house by the appellant was as licensee and not as tenant.

Thus the House of Lords emphasised that where parties contract on the terms of a written agreement, their legal relations are governed by the terms of that agreement, and not by unexpressed intentions or by surrounding circumstances.

2.2 *Street* v *Mountford*: the facts

Mr Street was the owner of a building known as 5 St Clements Gardens, Boscombe, Bournemouth. It was divided into furnished flatlets. On 7 March 1983 Mr Street and Mrs Mountford entered into a written agreement under which Mrs Mountford was given the right to occupy rooms 5 and 6 in the building. Although the agreement was taken in her name alone, she was orally permitted to share the rooms with her husband. In addition to the two rooms (one of which had its own cooking facilities) Mrs Mountford also had the sole use of a shower and lavatory. The terms of the written agreement were as follows:

I Mrs. Wendy Mountford agree to take from the owner Roger Street the single furnished room number 5 and 6 at 5 St. Clements Gardens, Boscombe, Bournemouth, commencing 7 March 1983 at a licence fee of £37 per week.

I understand that the right to occupy the above room is conditional on the strict observance of the following rules:

1.   No paraffin stoves, or other than the supplied form of heating, is allowed in the room.

2.   No one but the above-named person may occupy or sleep in the room without prior permission, and this personal licence is not assignable.

3.   The owner (or his agent) has the right at all times to enter the room to inspect its condition, read and collect money from meters, carry out maintenance works, install or replace furniture or for any other reasonable purpose.

4.   All rooms must be kept in a clean and tidy condition.

5.   All damage and breakages must be paid for or replaced at once. An initial deposit equivalent to 2 weeks licence fee will be refunded on termination of the licence subject to deduction for all damage or other breakages or arrears of licence fee, or retention towards the cost of any necessary possession proceedings.

6.   No nuisance or annoyance to be caused to the other occupiers. In particular, all music played after midnight to be kept low so as not to disturb occupiers of other rooms.

7.   No children or pets allowed under any circumstances whatsoever.

8.   Prompt payment of the licence fee must be made every Monday in advance without fail.

9.   If the licence fee or any part of it shall be seven days in arrear or if the occupier shall be in breach of any of the other terms of this agreement or if (except by arrangement) the room is left vacant or

unoccupied, the owner may re-enter the room and this licence shall then immediately be terminated (without prejudice to all other rights and remedies of the owner).

10. This licence may be terminated by 14 days' written notice given to the occupier at any time by the owner or his agent, or by the same notice by the occupier to the owner or his agent.

Occupier's signature

Owner/agent's signature

Date: 7 March 1983

I understand and accept that a licence in the above form does not and is not intended to give me a tenancy protected under the Rent Acts.

Occupier's signature.

On 12 August 1983, on Mrs Mountford's application, a fair rent was registered. Accordingly Mr Street applied to the county court for a declaration that Mrs Mountford was not a tenant but a licensee. There was no suggestion of misrepresentation, undue influence or non est factum, and no claim for rectification. In the county court Mr Recorder Rolf heard oral evidence. He held that apart from the heading and the footnote, the written agreement had all the hallmarks of a tenancy. Taken together with the fact that Mrs Mountford had exclusive occupation of the two rooms, and the fact that she and her husband behaved like tenants, he held that Mrs Mountford was a tenant, not a licensee.

2.3 *Street* v *Mountford*: construing the agreement

In the Court of Appeal (1984) 271 EG 1261, Slade LJ construed the written agreement. The principle of law which he expressed was that:

While the fact of exclusive occupation is a most important pointer as to the intentions of the parties their true intentions are the decisive consideration in determining whether an agreement creates a tenancy on the one hand or a licence on the other hand.

This proposition was soundly based on a long line of authority which has been reviewed in the preceding chapter. Moreover, it is consistent with the general approach of the courts to the construction of written agreements. In construing any contract the court is attempting to ascertain the intention of the parties to the contract. That intention is to be ascertained objectively, by ascertaining what intention a reasonable person would have had if placed in the situation of the parties. What the court must do is place itself in the same factual matrix as that of the parties. In so doing the court is entitled to take into account the surrounding circumstances with reference to which the words of the contract were used (*Reardon Smith Line Ltd* v *Hansen-Tangen* [1976] 3 All ER 570; *Prenn* v *Simmonds* [1971] 3 All ER 237). The question to be answered always is 'What is the meaning of what the parties have said' not, 'What did the parties mean to say', it being a presumption that the parties intended to say that which they have said (*Norton on Deeds*, 2nd edn p 50, approved by Lord Simon of Glaisdale in *L Schuler AG* v *Wickman Machine Tool Sales Ltd* [1974] AC 235).

Applying this approach, Slade LJ said of the written agreement:

Though it does not expressly so state, clause 3, in my opinion, shows that the right to occupy the premises conferred on the defendant was intended as an exclusive right of occupation in that it was thought necessary to give a special and express power to the plaintiff to enter. . . . With this exception, my own impression is quite the contrary [*sc to the recorder's view*]. The right conferred by the opening words of the document is not granted for any defined term and is described as a 'right to occupy', which is not apt to describe the right enjoyed by an ordinary tenant. Clause 2 which prohibits anyone except the defendant from occupying or sleeping in the premises without the plaintiff's prior permission and states 'this personal licence is not assignable', points to a licence rather than a tenancy. So too does clause 4: it would, I think, be most unusual to find a provision in a tenancy agreement obliging the tenant to keep his rooms in a 'tidy condition'. Clause 5, instead of placing an obligation on the plaintiff or defendant to repair, merely imposes on the defendant an obligation to pay for 'damage and breakages'. As to clause 7, which prohibits 'children and pets', I think that a provision prohibiting children would be very unusual in the context of a tenancy agreement. No less unusual in a tenancy agreement would be provisions in the precise form of clause 9, which gives the plaintiff power to re-enter if, among other circumstances, '(except by arrangement) the room is left vacant or unoccupied'. Furthermore, although I attach less importance to this point, the agreement contains none of the provisions which one commonly expects to find in tenancy agreements, such as provisions relating to repair, insurance and quiet possession. For these reasons, I think that, even if one disregards the declaration of intent at the very end of the agreement, its heading and reference to a 'licence fee' rather than rent, the agreement bears all the hallmarks of a licence, rather than a tenancy, save for the one important feature of exclusive occupation. With this exception, everything in the document itself points to the defendant being given a mere personal right to occupy the rooms, rather than a proprietary interest in them as tenant.

Slade LJ went on to say that the declaration of intent at the foot of the agreement could not be disregarded, and that it added strength to the conclusion that the true intention of the parties was to create a licence rather than a tenancy.

Although Slade LJ did not distinguish between exclusive occupation and exclusive possession, it is clear that he regarded Mrs Mountford as having been granted exclusive possession. Nevertheless, he did not find any difficulty in construing the agreement as a licence, even ignoring the declaration of intent. That this should be so demonstrates that the grant of exclusive possession is merely one of many factors from which the true intention of the parties is to be deduced. From a careful examination of the agreement as a whole, he concluded that the true intention of the parties was to create a licence. He did so by applying the new test introduced in the 1960's, namely whether the agreement was personal in its nature (see 1.4 above).

2.4 *Street* v *Mountford*: **exclussive possession restored**

In the House of Lords, it was not found necessary to construe the written agreement. Once it was found (in fact conceded) that Mrs Mountford had been granted exclusive possession, the House of Lords held that in the absence of special circumstances she was a tenant as a matter of law. The true intention of the parties was to be gathered not from the words of the written agreement but from the fact that exclusive possession had been granted. Lord Templeman, who delivered the only speech, criticised the analysis of the agreement carried out by Slade LJ as follows:

Slade LJ proceeded to analyse all the provisions of the agreement, not for the purpose of deciding whether his finding of exclusive possession was correct but for the purpose of assigning some of the provisions of the agreement to the category of terms which he thought are usually to be found in a tenancy agreement and of assigning other provisions to the category of terms which he thought are usually to be found in a licence. The Lord Justice may or may not have been right that in a letting of a furnished room it was 'most unusual to find a provision in a tenancy agreement obliging the tenant to keep his rooms in a "tidy condition"'. If the Lord Justice was right about this and other provisions there is still no logical method of evaluating the results of his survey. Slade LJ reached the conclusion that 'the agreement bears all the hallmarks of a licence, rather than a tenancy, save for the one important feature of exclusive occupation'. But in addition to the hallmark of exclusive occupation of residential accommodation there were the hallmarks of weekly payments for a periodical term. Unless these three hallmarks are decisive, it really becomes impossible to distinguish a contractual tenancy from a contractual licence save by reference to the professed intention of the parties or by the judge awarding marks for drafting.

Accordingly Lord Templeman concluded that where 'the only circumstances are that residential accommodation is offered and accepted with exclusive possession for a term at a rent, the result is a tenancy'.

2.5   Why construe the agreement?

Since it was common ground that Mrs Mountford had been granted exclusive possession, it was said to be 'unnecessary to analyse minutely the detailed rights and obligations contained in the agreement'. Indeed, save for the passage in which he criticises the analysis of Slade LJ, Lord Templeman does not refer to them at all. However, it is clear from his speech that he regarded it as permissible to construe an agreement dealing with the occupation of property only for the purpose of determining whether it confers exclusive possession upon the occupier. Hence the criticism of Slade LJ for construing the agreement 'not for the purpose of deciding whether his finding of exclusive possession was correct'. Similarly, in reviewing the earlier authorities, Lord Templeman described *Glenwood Lumber Co Ltd* v *Phillips* [1904] AC 405 as a case where:

The court after careful consideration of the purposes of the grant, the terms of the grant and the surrounding circumstances, came to the conclusion that the grant conferred exclusive possession and was *therefore* a tenancy [emphasis added].

So too *Addiscombe Garden Estates Ltd* v *Crabbe* [1959] 1 QB 513 was said to be a case where:

On analysis of the whole of the agreement the Court of Appeal came to the conclusion that the agreement conferred exclusive possession and *thus* created a tenancy [emphasis added].

It is clear from these passages that the objective of a court of construction is to determine whether or not the agreement to be construed does or does not confer exclusive possession on the occupier. Once that question has been answered, the status of the occupier follows as a matter of law. Accordingly the detailed provisions are only of relevance in so far as they assist in answering that question, and cannot be relied on in order to arrive at a general conclusion as to the intention of the parties.

2.6 Why is exclusive possession the test?

The features of the grant of exclusive possession were thus described by Lord Templeman:

The tenant possessing exclusive possession is able to exercise the rights of an owner of land, which is in the real sense his land albeit temporarily and subject to certain restrictions. A tenant armed with exclusive possession can keep out strangers and keep out the landlord unless the landlord is exercising limited rights reserved to him by the tenancy agreement to enter and view and repair. A licensee lacking exclusive possession can in no sense call the land his own and cannot be said to own any estate in the land.

The only right to which Lord Templeman expressly refers is the right to keep out strangers (including the landlord). However, this right is not a right of ownership, for an action in trespass may be maintained by any person in possession against any person who interferes with that possession. It is not necessary for the plaintiff to have an interest in the land because:

Possession gives the [occupier] a right against every man who cannot show a good title (*Roe d Haldane* v *Harvey* (1769) 4 Burr 2484 per Lord Mansfield CJ).

Moreover, there are many other rights which an owner has over his own land, such as the right to build upon it; the right to transfer it or create interests out of it; to burden it with incumbrances; if built upon to demolish the buildings and so on. The right to possession of land is one characteristic of the ownership of some interests in land, but there are interests which do not carry that right (eg reversionary interests or interests in incorporeal hereditaments). Since the crucial difference between a licence and a tenancy is that the former is not an interest in land but the latter is, it is not immediately clear why exclusive possession should be the distinction between them. The answer given by Lord Templeman was that:

No other test for distinguishing between a contractual tenancy and a contractual licence appears to be understandable or workable.

And again:

If exclusive possession at a rent for a term does not constitute a tenancy then the distinction between a contractual tenancy and a contractual licence of land becomes wholly unidentifiable.

Accordingly the rationale for the distinction appears to be one of expediency and practicality rather than any reason based upon legal analysis.

2.7 Is exclusive possession decisive?

Even though exclusive possession has been restored to its position of pre-eminence, it is still not decisive. As Lord Templeman said:

An occupier who enjoys exclusive possession is not necessarily a tenant. He may be owner in fee simple, a trespasser, a mortgagee in possession, an object of charity or a service occupier. To constitute a tenancy the occupier must be granted exclusive possession for a fixed or periodic term certain in consideration of a premium or periodical payments. The grant may be express, or may be inferred where the owner accepts weekly or other periodical payments from the occupier.

Exclusive possession alone is not enough. But is it enough if accompanied by the agreement of a term and the payment of a rent? In most cases, the answer will be yes. But there are cases where a different answer may be given. Thus even where an occupier enjoys exclusive possession in consideration for periodical payments, there are circumstances which negative the prima facie intention to create a tenancy. In the words of Lord Templeman:

> The intention to create a tenancy was negatived if the parties did not intend to enter into legal relationships at all, or where the relationship between the parties was that of vendor and purchaser master and service occupier, or where the owner, a requisitioning authority, had no power to grant a tenancy.

He also approved the dictum of Denning LJ in *Facchini* v *Bryson* [1952] 1 TLR 1386 (quoted in 1.7 above). He concluded:

> Henceforth the courts which have to deal with these problems will, save in exceptional circumstances, only be concerned to inquire whether as a result of an agreement relating to residential accommodation the occupier is a lodger or a tenant.

The status of contractual licensee seems to have disappeared.

2.8 The new approach

In summary, the new approach of the courts must be to ask the following questions:
(1) Did the parties intend to enter into legal relations?
(2) If so, has exclusive possession been conferred upon the occupier?
(3) Are there any special circumstances to negative the presumption that a tenancy has been created?
These elements must now be examined.

3 The New Approach: Stage One

3.1 Intention to create legal relations

A tenancy can only arise under a contract if the parties intend to enter into binding legal relations. If the parties do not intend to contract at all, the law will not impose a contract upon them. In *Booker* v *Palmer* [1942] 2 All ER 674 Lord Greene MR said:

There is one golden rule which is of very general application, namely, that the law does not impute intention to enter into legal relationships where the circumstances and the conduct of the parties negative any intention of the kind.

It is necessary to consider, therefore, what circumstances negative the intention to create legal relations.

3.2 Express declaration

In *Rose and Frank* v *Crompton* [1925] AC 445 the parties entered into an arrangement recorded in a memorandum. The memorandum provided:

This arrangement is not entered into nor is this memorandum written, as a formal or legal agreement . . . but is only a definite expression and record of the purpose and intention of the parties concerned, to which they each honourably pledge themselves.

Dishonourably, the arrangement was prematurely terminated. The House of Lords held that the memorandum gave rise to no legally enforceable obligation because of the 'honourable pledge' clause. Scrutton LJ said in the Court of Appeal:

It is quite possible for parties to come to an agreement by accepting a proposal with the result that the agreement does not give rise to legal relations. The reason of this is that the parties do not intend that their agreement shall give rise to legal relations. This intention may be implied from the subject matter of the agreement, but it may also be expressed by the parties.

In theory, therefore, it is open to parties to enter into a written agreement but to negative any intention to create legal relations by an express provision to that effect. In practice, however, it is unlikely that the court would uphold such a provision if all the other terms of the agreement were those of a tenancy. It is suggested that the court would adopt the same approach to such a clause as must now be adopted towards a clause which declares that the agreement is not intended to give rise to a tenancy. Lord Templeman put it thus in *Street* v *Mountford*:

> Words alone do not suffice. . . . The circumstances and the conduct of the parties show that what was intended was that the occupier should be granted exclusive possession at a rent for a term with a corresponding interest in the land which created a tenancy.

3.3   Family arrangements

Many family arrangements which bear all the signs of contracts are held not to give rise to legally enforceable obligations. Those agreements, or many of them, do not result in contracts at all even though there may be what between other parties would constitute consideration for the agreement. They are not contracts because the parties did not intend that they should be attended by legal consequences. Agreements such as these are outside the realm of contracts altogether (*Balfour* v *Balfour* [1919] 2 KB 571 per Scrutton LJ).

Thus in *Cobb* v *Lane* [1952] 1 All ER 1199 Miss Lane bought a house for her brother to occupy with his wife and daughter. In the first year he paid the rates, but never paid anything for his use or occupation of the house. The Court of Appeal held that he was a licensee only. This case was analysed by Lord Templeman in *Street* v *Mountford* as a case in which the conduct of the parties negatived any intention to enter into a contract at all. Similarly, in *Jones* v *Padavatton* [1969] 2 All ER 616 Mrs Jones bought a house for the occupation of her daughter, a Bar student. The arrangement was that the daughter was to live off the income derived from taking lodgers, and that Mrs Jones was to stop paying for her maintenance. The Court of Appeal held that the arrangement did not give rise to a legally binding contract, and that consequently the daughter was a mere licensee. Salmon LJ said:

> As a rule when arrangements are made between close relations, for example, between husband and wife, parent and child or uncle and nephew in relation to an allowance, there is a presumption against an intention of creating any legal relationship. This is not a presumption of law, but of fact. It derives from experience of life and human nature which shows that in such circumstances men and women usually do not intend to create legal rights and obligations, but intend to rely solely on family ties of mutual trust and affection.

The court adopted the same approach in *Horrocks* v *Foray* [1976] 1 All ER 737 where Mrs Foray failed to persuade the court that an arrangement under which her lover provided her and their child with a house to live in amounted to a legally enforceable contractual licence. Megaw LJ said:

> In order to establish a contract, whether it be an express contract or a contract implied by law, there has to be shown a meeting of the minds of the parties, with a definition of the contractual terms reasonably clearly made out, with an intention to effect the legal relationship; that is that the agreement that is made is one which is properly to be regarded as being enforceable by the court if one or the other party fails to comply with it; and it still remains a part of the law . . . that there must be consideration moving in order to establish a contract.

Scarman LJ agreed, saying that the arrangement could as well have been referable to the continuance of natural love and affection as to an intention to enter into an agreement which they intended to have legal effect.

3.4 Binding family arrangements

Nevertheless, there are cases in which the court has held a family arrangement to have legally binding consequences. The facts in *Errington* v *Errington and Woods* have already been set out (see 1.2 above). Denning LJ analysed the arrangement as follows:

> The father's promise was a unilateral contract—a promise of the house in return for their act of paying the instalments. It could not be revoked

by him once the couple entered on performance of the act, but it would cease to bind if they left it incomplete and unperformed, which they have not done.

In *Tanner* v *Tanner* [1975] 3 All ER 776 the court was able to find a contractual licence in circumstances where a man had persuaded his mistress to give up her protected tenancy in order to go to live in a house which he owned. Browne LJ and Brightman J found on the facts that the correct inference was that a contractual licence had been granted for consideration. Lord Denning MR put it in wider terms:

There was, it is true, no express contract to that effect, but the circumstances are such that the court should imply a contract by him—or, if need be, impose the equivalent of a contract by him— whereby they are entitled to have the use of the house as their home until the girls had finished school.

The notion of imposing a contract was repeated in *Hardwick* v *Johnson* [1978] 2 All ER 935. Mrs Hardwick bought a house for her son and daughter-in-law to live in. They agreed to pay her £7 per week, but the whole arrangement was very vague. Lord Denning MR said:

These family arrangements do have legal consequences; and, time and time again, the courts are called on to determine what is the true legal relationship resulting from them. . . . In most of these cases the question cannot be solved by looking to the intention of the parties, because the situation which arises is one which they never envisaged and for which they made no provision. ... The court has to look at all the circumstances and spell out the legal relationship. The court will pronounce in favour of a tenancy or a licence, a loan or a gift, or a trust, according to which legal relationship is most fitting in the situation which has arisen; and will find the terms of that relationship according to what reason and justice require.

The other two members of the court adopted a narrower basis for their decision and found that there was a contractual licence which Mrs Hardwick could not terminate as long as she continued to receive the agreed sum of £7 per week. The wider approach suffers from the same uncertainty as the test for distinguishing between a lease and a licence (is it personal in nature?) which prevailed in the Court of Appeal before the decision of the House of Lords in *Street* v *Mountford*. Reason and justice are somewhat subjective criteria, and it is to be hoped that in due course a more objective test will prevail.

3.5 Acts of generosity

Where the owner of land allows another to occupy it as an act of generosity, the court will not lightly assume that he intended to enter into legal relations. In *Booker* v *Palmer* [1942] 2 All ER 674 the owner of a cottage allowed it to be occupied rent free by a friend of a friend whose house had been destroyed by a bomb. He was said to have had the charitable intention to allow them to stay in the cottage for the duration of the war. Lord Greene MR said that an intention to create legal relations could not be imputed to him (see 3.1 above). He continued:

His sole motive was to act as a good and charitable citizen towards people in distress. In my opinion, the result is that the only permissible inference is that the appellant was intended to be there as licensee.

In *Marcroft Wagons Ltd* v *Smith* [1951] 2 KB 496 the owner of a house allowed the daughter of his deceased tenant to remain in the house because he had no immediate need for it. It was held by the Court of Appeal that despite the fact that the occupier paid rent to the landlord no tenancy had been created. Sir Raymond Evershed MR said:

Landlords who may have ordinary human instincts of kindliness and courtesy, may often be afraid to allow a tenant the benefit of those natural instincts in case it may afterwards turn out that the tenant has thereby acquired a position from which he cannot subsequently be dislodged. In the general interest, it may be necessary that the relationship should have to assume a much more formal character than would otherwise be necessary; nevertheless, I should be extremely sorry if anything which fell from this court were to have the effect that a landlord could never grant to a person in the position of the defendant any kind of indulgence particularly in circumstances such as existed . . . when the defendant lost her mother.

Against the background of the 'indulgence' he concluded that a licence had been created. In the light of *Street* v *Mountford* this case should now be analysed as a case in which there was no intention to create legal relations.

A case of the same category is *Heslop* v *Burns* [1974] 3 All ER 406 where Stamp LJ said:

> On the facts of this case it is, in my judgement, abundantly clear that the parties did not enter into any arrangement, far less any arrangement intended to create a legal relationship, as to the terms on which the defendants should occupy the property. There was no contract, no arrangement, no statement by the deceased. The defendants were allowed to move into the property and occupy it simply as a result of the bounty of the deceased and without any arrangements as to the terms on which they should do so.

3.6 Holding over

Where an occupier of land holds over after the termination of an interest, and makes periodical payments to the owner, the question often arises whether a tenancy has arisen by the payment and acceptance of rent. It seems now that the question to be asked is whether the parties intended to enter into a contractual relationship with each other, or whether they did not intend legal consequences to flow from their conduct. In *Marcroft Wagons Ltd* v *Smith* (above) Denning LJ adopted this approach. He said:

> If the acceptance of rent can be explained on some other footing than that a contractual tenancy existed, as, for instance, by reason of an existing or possible statutory right to remain, then a new tenancy should not be inferred.

In such circumstances the owner's conduct in accepting rent is to be attributed to an intention to recognise rights and obligations arising under a contract which has already been made, and not to an intention to make a new contract. Similarly the owner may explain his acceptance of rent as having been occasioned by a mistake on the part of his agent (*Clarke* v *Grant* [1950] 1 KB 104) or his computer (*Legal and General Assurance Society Ltd* v *General Metal Agencies Ltd* (1969) 20 P & CR 953). This seems to be an exception to the general law of contract, because a unilateral mistake (unless known to the other party) does not normally give rise to any legal consequence. Moreover, whether parties have or have not entered into a contract is usually determined objectively, not subjectively.

By the same token, where the occupier himself asserts some statutory right to remain, the payment of rent by him will be attributed to an intention to comply with his pre-existing obligations, and not to an intention to assume new ones (*Lewis* v *MTC (Cars) Ltd* [1975] 1 All ER 874).

The most liberal approach was that adopted by Ormrod LJ in the most recent of the holding over cases, *Longrigg, Burrough & Trounson* v *Smith* (1979) 251 EG 847 in which he said:

The old common law presumption of a tenancy from the payment and acceptance of a sum in the nature of rent dies very hard. But I think the authorities make it quite clear that in these days of statutory controls over the landlord's rights of possession, this presumption is unsound and no longer holds. The question now is a purely open question; it is simply: is it right and proper to infer from all the circumstances of the case, including the payments, that the parties had reached an agreement for a tenancy? I think it does not now go any further than that.

The important question is whether the parties can be said to have reached an agreement at all. If they are found to have reached a genuine agreement, it is likely that such an agreement will be held to give rise to a tenancy.

3.7   Agreements 'subject to contract'

One way in which parties may indicate that they do not yet intend to enter into binding legal relations is to state that negotiations are 'subject to contract' or 'subject to lease'. The effect of such a stipulation is that the parties will not be bound until the exchange of formal contracts or lease and counterpart as the case may be. Even where negotiations are not expressly stated to be 'subject to contract' that qualification may be implied. Thus where parties are negotiating for the grant of a lease, which they contemplate will be completed by exchange of lease and counterpart, any apparent agreement in correspondence will be treated as conditional upon exchange of lease and counterpart (*Leveson* v *Parfum Marcel Rochas (England) Ltd* (1966) 200 EG 407). Even if the proposed tenant is let into possession during the course of the negotiations, they remain 'subject to contract' (*D'Silva* v *Lister House Development Ltd* [1971] Ch 17 at 29).

In such circumstances it is suggested that the status of the occupier is likely to be that of licensee. In *Isaac* v *Hotel de Paris Ltd* [1960] 1 All ER 348 Mr Isaac was negotiating to buy the share capital of Hotel de Paris Ltd which owned a lease of the Parisian Hotel in Port of Spain, Trinidad. In the course of the negotiations he was installed in the hotel for the purpose of managing a night bar on behalf of the company. At a subsequent meeting terms were agreed 'subject to contract' under which Mr Isaac was to remain in occupation, running the night bar on his own account, and would pay the outgoings of the hotel including the rent. Mr Isaac was also to pay the balance of the purchase price for the shares. The Privy Council held that he was a licensee. Lord Denning said:

The circumstances and the conduct of the parties show that all that was intended was that the appellant should have a personal privilege of running a night bar on the premises, with no interest in the land at all. It was at first only a privilege to be there pending the execution of a formal contract. Later, when the contract fell through, and notice was given to him to remove his belongings, even that privilege came to an end.

In *Street* v *Mountford* Lord Templeman described the case as one:

in which the parties did not intend to enter into contractual relationships unless and until the negotiations 'subject to contract' were replaced by a binding contract.

It is suggested that where parties are negotiating for the grant of a formal lease, their intention is almost always that any contract between them is to be contained in that lease. The last thing they are likely to intend is the grant of a periodic tenancy containing no terms at all other than those implied by law. However, in *D'Silva* v *Lister House Development Ltd* (above) Buckley J held that the entry into possession of the proposed tenant and the payment of one quarter's rent created a periodic tenancy. The judge reached this conclusion even though he held that the parties were negotiating for the grant of a formal lease, and that those negotiations remained 'subject to contract'. It is submitted that this part of the case was wrongly decided.

4 The New Approach: Stage Two

4.1 Exclusive possession

There can be no tenancy unless the occupier of the property in question has exclusive possession (*Street* v *Mountford* per Lord Templeman). It is the grant of exclusive possession which enables the tenant temporarily to exercise at least some of the rights over land which belong to an owner of it. Accordingly the second stage in the inquiry is to ask whether the contract confers exclusive possession on the occupier.

4.2 What is exclusive possession?

In *Street* v *Mountford* Mrs Mountford (and her husband) were the only occupiers of the property comprised in the written agreement. The agreement gave to Mr Street:

The right at all times to enter the room to inspect its condition, read and collect money from meters, carry out maintenance works, install or replace furniture or *for any other reasonable purpose* [emphasis added].

Despite the apparent width of this right, Lord Templeman described it as 'the limited rights of inspection and maintenance and the like', and it was conceded by counsel for Mr Street that Mrs Mountford had been granted exclusive possession. However, it is important to distinguish between exclusive occupation of property, and exclusive possession of it. This distinction may have been lost sight of in *Street* v *Mountford*. Thus in *E Moss Ltd* v *Brown* [1946] 2 All ER 557 the tenant of a flat allowed friends to stay in it, making weekly payments. She kept some of her belongings there, and went back from time to time to fetch things. However she did not expect to be put up there except by arrangement. Somervell LJ considered that (even though the tenant's friends were the sole occupiers of the flat) exclusive possession had not been granted.

In *Cobb* v *Lane* [1952] 1 All ER 1199 Somervell LJ referred to earlier cases where:

> it was clearly intended that the person who occupied the premises should have the possession which normally people have in their homes. Those cases show that exclusive possession is not a test negativing the possibility of the occupier's being a licensee. If you use the expression 'exclusive possession' as meaning the rights which a tenant has against his landlord, then, of course, it might well be that an admission of that would lead to the conclusion arrived at in *Lynes* v *Snaith* [ie that exclusive possession is inconsistent with a licence].

This formulation does not, however, define the test otherwise than in a circular fashion. If the existence of a tenancy is dependent on the grant of exclusive possession, and exclusive possession is described as the rights which a tenant has against his landlord, we are no further forward. Stamp LJ gave a more helpful description in *Heslop* v *Burns* [1974] 3 All ER 406 at 410:

> It may, as I see it, be used to mean that, as a factual matter, the occupant, alone or together with his family, occupies the premises and does not share them with any other person. Such a situation is not inconsistent with the occupation being enjoyed under a mere licence. Or the expression may be used to mean that the occupant has a right to exclude the owner from the premises. . . . Where the expression is used in the latter sense as describing a situation where the occupier has the right to exclude the owner it is clearly more difficult to reconcile it with the existence of a mere licence to occupy.

It is suggested that much confusion would be avoided if the first sense were called 'exclusive occupation' and only the latter sense were called 'exclusive possession'.

4.3   Non-exclusive occupation

In some cases a person occupying land will not be the sole person in occupation. Where this is so, plainly he cannot be a tenant, for he has no right to exclude other occupiers from the property, let alone the owner.

Thus, in *Bahamas International Trust Co Ltd* v *Threadgold* [1974]

3 All ER 881 Mr Threadgold was allowed to live in a farmhouse rent and rates free, and to retain his cows and other livestock on eleven acres of grazing land. Mr Threadgold claimed that his licence took effect as a tenancy by virtue of s 2(1) of the Agricultural Holdings Act 1948. The House of Lords held that it did not. Lord Diplock construed the grant of the right to 'retain' cows on the land as indicating that the cows referred to were those on the land at the date of the agreement together with any progeny born to them during the term of the licence. Mr Threadgold was not entitled to put fresh livestock on the land. Thus Lord Diplock concluded:

As a matter of construction I see nothing in the words which either expressly or by necessary implication gives to Mr Threadgold any right to exclude the freeholders from the land or the farm buildings or to stop them from making whatever use they please of the land or buildings so long as that use does not prevent his reasonable exercise of the rights conferred on him by the licence.

Accordingly it was not possible for the grant to take effect as a tenancy, because a licence to occupy land within the meaning of s 2(1) of the Agricultural Holdings Act 1948 has to confer upon the grantee an exclusive right to prevent the grantor and any other person authorised by the grantor from making any use of the land, at least for agricultural purposes.

4.4 The sharing cases reconsidered

The cases which considered agreements to share residential accommodation have been discussed in the context of the law before *Street* v *Mountford* (see 1.8 above). Lord Templeman dealt with these cases in a passage whose true meaning is difficult to assess. Having set out the facts of *Somma* v *Hazlehurst* (see 1.8 above) he continued:

Although the Rent Acts must not be allowed to alter or influence the construction of an agreement, the court should, in my opinion, be astute to detect and frustrate sham devices and artificial transactions whose only object is to disguise the grant of a tenancy and to evade the Rent Acts. I would disapprove of the decision in this case ... and for the same reason would disapprove of the decision in *Aldrington Garages Ltd* v *Fielder* ... and *Sturolson & Co* v *Weniz* ....

It is possible to interpret this passage in a number of ways.

(1) It may be that Lord Templeman merely intended to disapprove the three cases on their facts. Each case was a case where the sharers knew each other before they entered into the sharing agreement, and where it was part of their intention to share the accommodation *together*. However whether a transaction is a sham is essentially a question of fact. In *Somma* v *Hazlehurst* it was not argued that the transaction was a sham; in *Aldrington Garages Ltd* v *Fielder* one sharer left, leaving the other in occupation but paying only half the aggregate consideration payable by both sharers, and in *Sturolson & Co* v *Weniz* the Court of Appeal held that the parties intended to be bound by the written agreement which they all signed and that consequently the written agreement was not a sham. Nevertheless it is unusual for the House of Lords to overrule decisions of the Court of Appeal on questions of fact.

(2) Lord Templeman may have intended to lay down a general rule of public policy outlawing commercial agreements for the sharing of residential property. In *Somma* v *Hazlehurst* Cumming-Bruce LJ said:

> We can see no reason why an ordinary landlord . . . should not be able to grant a licence to occupy an ordinary house. If that is what both he and the licensee intend and if they can frame any written agreement in such a way as to demonstrate that it is not really an agreement for a lease masquerading as a licence, we can see no reason in law or justice why they should be prevented from achieving that object. Nor can we see why their common intentions should be categorised as bogus or unreal or as sham merely on the grounds that the court disapproves of the bargain.

And in *Sturolson & Co* v *Weniz* Fox LJ said:

> It is clear that, notwithstanding the Rent Acts, there is no reason, as a matter of public policy, why a landlord should not grant a licence to occupy a dwelling house so that the transaction is outside the protection of the Rent Acts.

Lord Templeman may have intended to lay down a new rule of public policy precisely contrary to the general statements made in the Court of Appeal. If so, he has responded to a suggestion made by Mr Megarry QC nearly twenty years ago in *The Rent Acts* (10th edn) p 60:

It is difficult to see how the challenge can be met save by evolving some new doctrine that, on grounds of public policy or otherwise, a purported licence will in fact create a tenancy if the circumstances require this eg, if, but for the Rent Acts, it is probable (or, perhaps, virtually certain) that a tenancy and not a licence would have been created.

A rule of public policy to this effect would leave it open to parties to enter into a sharing agreement where there were genuine reasons, unconnected with rent control and security of tenure, for doing so.

(3) Lord Templeman may have meant to extend into a new sphere of law the approach to tax avoidance schemes which has been evolving in the House of Lords, culminating in *Furniss* v *Dawson* [1984] 1 All ER 530. If so, the court will be able to disregard any transaction whose purpose is avoidance of statutory control, even if the transaction is not a sham. A transaction of this kind might well fall into the second of the phrases used by Lord Templeman, viz 'artificial transactions'.

Until such time as the implications of this part of Lord Templeman's speech have been explored by the courts, it is plainly unwise for any property owner to seek to allow persons to occupy property on the terms of a 'sharing agreement' at least where the arrangement is made at arm's length.

4.5 Exclusive possession negatived by nature of the right

In some cases the nature of the property which is the subject matter of the grant may be such that exclusive possession is negatived. In *Clore* v *Theatrical Properties Ltd* [1936] 3 All ER 483 the parties entered into a grant of front of house rights in a theatre. The document was described as a lease; it contained a covenant against assignment and a right of re-entry. Nevertheless the Court of Appeal held that it created a licence. By contrast in *Piper* v *Muggleton* [1956] 2 QB 569 Mrs Piper was held to be a tenant of half a shop, the remainder being used by her landlord, Bert Muggleton. Jenkins LJ said:

We do not think the possibility of a tenancy is negatived by the circumstance that the area between the applicant's part and the counter standing on the respondent's part was used in common by themselves and their respective customers as a means of access, and served also as a way through to the respondent's living room at the back of the shop, nor do we think that a tenancy is necessarily negatived by the circumstance that the respondent kept the key of the door leading into the shop from the street.

There are nowadays many shops and stores which are occupied in small units. The mere fact that the units are within a larger unit controlled by the owner will not prevent tenancies from being created, at least where the units themselves are individually delineated and lockable. An establishment of this kind was considered by Fox J in *Ross Auto Wash Ltd* v *Herbert* (1978) 250 EG 971. Although the issue in that case was directed to the question of occupation for the purposes of Part II of the Landlord and Tenant Act 1954, it is suggested that the traders in the individual stalls were clearly licensees.

4.6 Lodgers

The classic description of a lodger was that by Blackburn J in *Allan* v *Liverpool Overseers* (1874) LR 9 QB 180 at 191:

A lodger in a house, although he has the exclusive use of rooms in the house, in the sense that nobody else is to be there, and though his goods are stowed there, yet he is not in exclusive occupation in that sense, because the landlord is there for the purpose of being able, as landlords commonly do in the case of lodgings, to have his own servants to look after the house and the furniture, and has retained to himself the occupation, though he has agreed to give the exclusive enjoyment of the occupation to the lodger.

This passage demonstrates clearly the difference in kind between exclusive occupation (or exclusive enjoyment) on the one hand and exclusive possession on the other. What negatives exclusive possession is the fact that the landlord requires a high degree of control over the property in order to be able to perform his part of the bargain, ie the provision of services. This position is to be contrasted with more limited rights of entry for the purposes of inspection and repair.

Thus in *Appah* v *Parncliffe Investments Ltd* [1964] 1 All ER 838 a house was divided into seventeen rooms, each with its own lock. No meals were provided, but the rooms were cleaned daily and bed linen was changed weekly. The rooms each had cooking facilities in the shape of a gas ring. Mrs Appah occupied one such room as her residence. The Court of Appeal held that she was a lodger. Similarly, in *Marchant* v *Charters* (the facts of which are set out in 1.4 above) the occupier was held to be a licensee. In *Street* v *Mountford* Lord Templeman said that the decision was sustainable on the ground that the occupier was a lodger and did not enjoy exclusive possession. A person may be a lodger even though his lodgings are let to him unfurnished. In *Abbeyfield (Harpenden) Society Ltd* v *Woods* [1968] 1 All ER 352 Mr Woods was the sole occupier of a single room in an old people's home. The 'rent' included two main meals a day, and the cost of heating, lighting and other outgoings. However, Mr Woods provided his own furniture. He was held to be a licensee. In *Street* v *Mountford* Lord Templeman described the case as one in which the occupier was held to be a lodger and therefore a licensee rather than a tenant. Cases to the same effect are *Luganda* v *Service Hotels Ltd* [1969] 2 Ch 209 (a furnished serviced room) and *R* v *South Middlesex Rent Tribunal ex parte Beswick* (1976) 32 P & CR 67 (a room in a YWCA hostel). It is likely that these cases should now be seen as cases of lodgers, and that the court will be prepared to hold that a person is a lodger where he occupies furnished serviced accommodation, or where he is provided with meals, or where the accommodation carries with it the provision of communal facilities.

4.7 Serviced commercial accommodation

Although the expression 'lodger' is only appropriate to one who occupies residential accommodation, it is suggested that similar principles apply to occupation of commercial property, where the owner requires a high degree of control in order to perform his part of the bargain. The facts of *Taylor* v *Caldwell* are set out in 1.6 above. Shortly, the grantor was to provide a wide variety of entertainments for the grand concerts to be organised by the grantee. A high degree of control would have been necessary in order to do so, and accordingly the court readily concluded that the grant was that of a licence only. Similarly in *Ross Auto Wash Ltd* v *Herbert* (1978) 250 EG 971 stallholders were provided with a wide variety of services, including the running of individual stalls during the licensee's occasional absences, provision of credit card facilities and so on. It is suggested that the assumption that they were truly licensees was correct.

The provision of services or attendance on the property should of course be distinguished from the common case where the landlord recovers the cost of repair and maintenance of the structure and common parts of a building through a so-called service charge.

4.8   Service occupiers

A service occupier is another category of person who, though in sole physical occupation of property, does not have exclusive possession of it. His occupation is treated as representative of his employer. The essential feature of a service occupancy is that the occupier is required to occupy the property in question for the better performance of his duties. Thus where a master rope-maker was given the right to live in a house in Chatham dockyard as part payment for his services it was held that he occupied it beneficially and not in a representative capacity (*Hughes* v *Chatham Overseers* (1843) 5 Man & G 54). By contrast the surgeon of Greenwich Hospital who was in occupation of a house at the infirmary of the hospital appropriated to the surgeon was held to be in representative occupation (*Dobson* v *Jones* (1844) 5 Man & G 112). In *Smith* v *Seghill Overseers* (1875) LR 10 QB 422 a colliery company provided a number of houses for its workmen and allocated the houses at their discretion, giving preference to married men. A workman was not bound to live in any of the houses. The workmen were held to be in beneficial, not representative, occupation. Mellor J said:

The governing principle is that, in order to constitute an occupation as a servant, it must be an occupation ancillary to the performance of the duties which the occupier has engaged to perform.

Applying these principles, a bank manager required to live over the bank (*Tennant* v *Smith* [1892] AC 150), a Methodist minister required to live in a manse (*Reed* v *Cattermole* [1937] 1 KB 613) and a police officer required to live in a police house (*Langley* v *Appleby* [1976] 3 All ER 391) have all been held to be service occupiers. A modern statement of the test is that of Lord Upjohn in *Northern Ireland Commr of Valuation* v *Fermanagh Protestant Board of Education* [1969] 3 All ER 352, where he said:

First, if it is essential to the performance of the duties of the occupying servant that he should occupy the particular house, or it may be a house within a closely defined perimeter, then, being established that this is the mutual understanding of the master and the servant, the occupation . . . is that of the master and not of the servant. . . . Secondly, there is the case where it is not essential for the servant to occupy a particular house or to live within a particular perimeter, but by doing so he can better perform his duties as servant to a material degree: then in such case, if there is an express term in the contract between master and servant that he shall so reside, the occupation . . . is treated as the occupation of the master and not of the servant.

Accordingly, there are two alternative tests to determine whether an occupier is a service occupier. Either the occupation is necessary in order for the duties to be performed at all (eg a resident caretaker) or alternatively the contract of employment contains a residence requirement, and the residence in fact assists the better performance of the employee's duties to a material degree.

4.9 Exclusive possession negatived by express terms

The terms of the agreement may themselves expressly state that possession remains vested in the owner. Although occupation may be shared by many people, possession is indivisible. Accordingly, if possession remains vested in the owner, it follows that it cannot have been transferred to the occupier. In *Shell-Mex and BP Ltd* v *Manchester Garages Ltd* [1971] 1 All ER 841 the plaintiff allowed the defendant to trade from a petrol filling station on the terms of a written agreement. The agreement contained a provision in the following terms:

Not to impede in any way the officers servants or agents of the [plaintiff] in the exercise by them of the [plaintiff's] rights of possession and control of the premises.

All three members of the Court of Appeal held that that clause was inconsistent with the grant of a tenancy. Sachs LJ said that it was 'of its own substance . . . fatal to the . . . contention' that the agreement created a tenancy. Buckley LJ said it was:

consistent only with the fact that this transaction was in truth a licence transaction and not a tenancy under which the defendants would obtain an exclusive right to possession of the property during the term of the tenancy, subject of course to any rights reserved by the plaintiffs.

This case appears to have been referred to with approval by Lord Templeman in *Street* v *Mountford*, although the reasoning of Lord Denning MR, the third member of the court (based upon the personal nature of the transaction) was disapproved. It is likely, therefore that this decision remains good law. It would be dangerous, however, to suppose that an express provision stating that possession remains vested in the grantor will necessarily prevent an arrangement from being a tenancy. In the wake of *Street* v *Mountford* the court is likely to scrutinise such provisions more sceptically than heretofore.

Where the terms of the grant do not give the grantee unlimited use of the property, that may be an indication that a licence has been created. Thus in *Manchester City Council* v *National Car Parks Ltd* (1981) 262 EG 1297 the defendant had been granted a right to use a piece of land:

during the licence term between the hours of 00.01 and 02.00 hours and 07.00 and 24.00 hours daily for the purposes of a public vehicle park and for no other purpose whatsoever.

Lawton LJ (with whom Templeman LJ agreed) said:

It seems to me that that clause, on the face of it, did not grant, and was not intended to grant exclusive possession of the land.

However, the mere fact that use of the property is confined to limited hours does not necessarily negative exclusive possession. Thus in *Joel* v *International Circus and Christmas Fair* (1924) 124 LT 459 a stallholder at a fair was held to be a tenant even though the owners had the right to revise or alter the dates of opening or closing. Equally, in *Westminster Corpn* v *Southern Railway* [1936] AC 511 Lord Russell said that the operator of a railway bookstall could be a tenant even though access to the bookstall was limited to the hours during which the railway station was open. Moreover it is not uncommon to find that a lease of office accommodation prohibits use outside normal office hours.

A provision entitling the owner to require the occupier to

move from one place to another (eg from one stall to another) is probably a term which would be inconsistent with the grant of exclusive possession. And a right to compel the occupier to share accommodation has been said to be 'wholly inconsistent' with exclusive possession (*Somma* v *Hazlehurst* [1978] 2 All ER 1011 at 1022) although the particular agreement construed in that case has since been castigated as a sham (*Street* v *Mountford*).

4.10 Pointers to exclusive possession

An agreement on the part of the occupier to permit the owner to enter the property for limited purposes is a pointer towards exclusive possession, for it would be unnecessary if the occupier was not entitled to exclude the owner (*The Three D's Co Ltd* v *Barrow* (1949) 154 EG 145; *Facchini* v *Bryson* [1952] 1 TLR 1386). So too is an express prohibition against subletting, since only a person with exclusive possession is in a position to confer it upon another (*Facchini* v *Bryson*). Other terms which have been held to point towards exclusive possession include a covenant for quiet enjoyment of the premises (because by such a covenant the owner binds himself not to disturb the occupier's enjoyment) and a right of re-entry on breach of obligation (because it predicates that the grantor has already parted with possession) (*Addiscombe Garden Estates Ltd* v *Crabbe* [1957] 1 QB 513).

Analyses of detailed written agreements in earlier cases often contain indications that particular terms are more 'appropriate' to a licence than a tenancy (eg *Somma* v *Hazlehurst* [1978] 2 All ER 1011; *Aldrington Garages Ltd* v *Fielder* (1978) 37 P & CR 461). Such statements should be treated with caution in the light of Lord Templeman's strictures in *Street* v *Mountford* (see 2.6 above).

4.11 Management agreements and partnerships

Owners of commercial and agricultural property often enter into commercial arrangements with an intended trader, which carry with them a right to use particular property. By this means they hope to avoid granting exclusive possession. Thus in *Harrison-Broadley* v *Smith* [1964] 1 All ER 867 a landowner entered into a partnership with a working farmer. Each party contributed to the partnership capital; the farmer was to work the land, and the profits and losses were to be shared one tenth to the landowner and nine tenths to the farmer. The farmer's right to work the land was held to be a non-exclusive licence. Accordingly it did not take effect as a tenancy under s 2(1) of the Agricultural Holdings Act 1948. Harman LJ said:

> This is not, I think, really a licence to the partnership, because I cannot give myself a licence, and I think I cannot give myself a licence jointly with someone else, for I already have a right to go on the land, and it is tautologous to talk of myself as allowing myself to go on my own property.

On the facts of that case it is clear that the landowner was involved in the farming business, and was undertaking some business risk. Where the business risk is absent the result may well be different. So in *Teasdale* v *Walker* [1958] 3 All ER 307 Mrs Teasdale purported to employ Nathan Glassman as the manager of her shop in Skegness. Mr Glassman paid £750 for his appointment, and his remuneration was to:

> consist of the whole of the profits of the business except the said sum of £750 and the manager shall have full liberty to conduct the business of the employer in whatever manner he thinks fit without any hindrance or interference on the part of the employer.

The Court of Appeal held that the agreement was a sham. Pearce LJ said:

> So far as it is alleged that the tenant was the employer and Mr Glassman was her manager, it seems to us that it was a mere fiction. She had no control whatever over Mr Glassman's method of conducting the business. She had expressly agreed not to interfere. She had no interest in the financial result. She had received her £750; and whether he made a profit or loss did not concern her. . . . The plain effect of it was that she had sold to him for £750 the right to occupy the premises for his mock auctions for a year . . . and he took over all liability in respect of outgoings during that year.

Accordingly, the court held that Mrs Teasdale was not in occupation of the premises for the purposes of Part II of the Landlord and Tenant Act 1954. It was not necessary for the court to consider whether Mr Glassman was a tenant, but it seems from the tenor of the judgement of the court that he had exclusive possession. Indeed Pearce LJ referred to the case of *Bobbio* v *Watney Combe & Reid* (13 July 1955, unreported) where Parker LJ said that a somewhat similar arrangement 'was a subterfuge to avoid a breach of covenant against sub-letting and parting with possession, and that it clearly amounted to parting with possession'. A similar conclusion was reached in *Wang* v *Wei* (1976) 237 EG 657 where the 'manager' of a Chinese restaurant was held to be in truth a tenant. The management agreement was held to be a sham as both parties had treated it as a tenancy. It is suggested that the vital feature of a true management agreement is that the proprietor of the business remains financially interested in its prosperity and is exposed to real business risk.

5 The New Approach: Stage Three

5.1 The search for special circumstances

Once it is established that the parties intended to enter into legal relations and that exclusive possession has been conferred upon the occupier, the court will hold that the occupier is a tenant, unless there are special circumstances to displace that conclusion. In *Street* v *Mountford* Lord Templeman said:

Legal relationships to which the grant of exclusive possession might be referable and which would or might negative the grant of an estate or interest in the land include occupancy under a contract for the sale of the land, occupancy pursuant to a contract of employment or occupancy referable to the holding of an office.

It is suggested that this passage is a little misleading. Where a person is in occupation of land pursuant to a contract of employment or because he holds an office, he is likely to be a service occupier. And as we have seen, in the eyes of the law the occupation of a service occupier is representative of his employer (see 4.8 above). Accordingly, it is suggested that such occupiers do not have exclusive possession at all. Nevertheless, there are clearly special circumstances which can assist in negativing a tenancy.

5.2 Incapacity to grant a tenancy

A series of cases decided during the Second World War established the principle that where a requisitioning authority permitted persons to occupy requisitioned property, no tenancy was created because the requisitioning authority did not itself have any estate or interest in the property (see eg *Minister of*

Health v *Belotti* [1944] KB 298; *Southgate BC* v *Watson* [1944] KB 541; *Ministry of Agriculture* v *Matthews* [1950] 1 KB 148). So an agreement which gave a farmer the right to exclusive possession of part of a former RAF airfield for agricultural purposes was held to create a licence (*Finbow* v *Air Ministry* [1963] 2 All ER 647). These cases seem to be an exception to the general rule that as between landlord and tenant a tenancy by estoppel can arise even where the grantor has no interest in the land he has purported to demise. The reason for the exception may be that the requisitioning authority's powers derive from statute, and parties cannot ordinarily enlarge statutory powers by estoppel. However, this principle has been extended into the sphere of private rights. In *Torbett* v *Faulkner* [1952] 2 TLR 659, Mr Torbett bought a house for the occupation of a prospective employee of a company which he proposed to form. The company paid the employee's salary, but made a deduction from it for the house. Denning LJ said:

I would point out that Mr Faulkner seems to have occupied the house under an agreement with the company and not with Mr Torbett personally. Now the company had no estate or interest in the land at all. It had nothing out of which it could carve a tenancy. It was in this respect in the same position as a requisitioning authority. It could only grant a licence and not a tenancy. This is another reason for holding Mr Faulkner to be a licensee only.

In the context of a claim for possession by the true owner of the property the grantor's lack of title to grant a tenancy is plainly relevant. However if the grantor claims possession he would be estopped from relying upon his own lack of capacity to grant a tenancy (cf *Stratford* v *Syrett* [1958] 1 QB 107). It may be doubted therefore whether the first set of exceptional circumstances is likely to be of practical importance.

5.3   Occupation under a contract for sale

In *Howard* v *Shaw* (1841) 8 M & W 118 a person was let into exclusive possession under a contract for purchase. Two of the judges held that he was a tenant at will, but Lord Abinger said that while he occupied under a valid contract for the sale of the property he could not be considered as a tenant. And in *Walters*

v *Roberts* (1980) 41 P & CR 210 Nourse J held that a purchaser
let into occupation under a contract did not have a licence
capable of taking effect as a tenancy under s 2(1) of the
Agricultural Holdings Act 1948. This approach seems to have
been approved by Lord Templeman in *Street* v *Mountford* (see 5.1
above). Most contracts for the sale of land make specific
provision for the status of a purchaser let into occupation prior
to completion. Commonly the purchaser is declared to be the
'licensee and not the tenant' of the vendor, and is required to
pay interest on the purchase price. It is likely that in such
circumstances the purchaser does not acquire exclusive
possession at all. But even where he does, it is unlikely that a
tenancy will result (cf *Dunthorne and Shaw* v *Wiggins* [1943] 2 All
ER 678). But where a purchaser is let into occupation under an
arrangement separate from the contract of sale and pays for his
use and occupation, a tenancy may be created (*Francis Jackson
Development Ltd* v *Stempt* [1943] 2 All ER 601).

Finally it should be noted that even if the occupier is not a
tenant, he may have limited security from eviction, if the
property in question is a dwelling house. Under s 88 of the
Housing Act 1980, where under the terms of a rental purchase
agreement a person has been let into possession of a dwelling
house, the court has wide powers to adjourn possession
proceedings and to suspend possession orders or postpone the
date of possession. A 'rental purchase agreement' is an
agreement for the purchase of a dwelling house under which the
whole or part of the purchase price is payable in three or more
instalments, and completion is deferred until the whole or a
specified part of the purchase price has been paid (s 88(4)).

5.4 Temporary arrangements

It is not clear whether the fact that parties envisage that
occupation will be temporary only is a factor tending to negative
the inference that a tenancy has been created. In *Eastleigh BC* v
Walsh (19 November 1984, unreported) the Court of Appeal was
prepared to hold that the grant of 'emergency shelter' amounted
to a licence rather than a tenancy. Although their decision was
reversed by the House of Lords ([1985] 2 All ER 112), the House
of Lords decided the case purely as a matter of construction of an

unambiguous written agreement. Had the agreement been equivocal, the temporary nature of the arrangement might have assumed more significance. Thus in *Manchester City Council* v *National Car Parks Ltd* (1981) 262 EG 1297 one of the factors which persuaded the Court of Appeal that a licence had been created was the fact that the land in question was a city centre site being held for development, thus giving rise to a 'good commercial reason' why the grantor did not want to grant a tenancy. However, it is suggested that if the prospect of redevelopment is the only factor, a tenancy is unlikely to be negatived. Since many licences are granted of sites being held for development, and many people occupy 'short life' housing, this problem is likely to come before the courts before very long.

5.5   Acts of friendship or generosity

In *Facchini* v *Bryson* [1952] 1 TLR 1386 Denning LJ said:

In all the cases where an occupier has been held to be a licensee there has been something in the circumstances, such as a family arrangement, an act of friendship or generosity, or such like, to negative any intention to create a tenancy.

Lord Templeman in *Street* v *Mountford* treated this dictum as referring to 'the special circumstances which are capable of negativing an intention to create a tenancy'. In so doing, Lord Templeman must have been envisaging these circumstances being weighed in the balance at the third stage of the enquiry. However, as we have seen, most of these circumstances arise where the parties do not intend to enter into legal relations at all.

One of the few cases in which a contract conferring exclusive possesion on the occupier has been held to amount to a licence is *Errington* v *Errington and Woods* [1952] 1 KB 290. That case was described by Lord Templeman as having 'exceptional circumstances'. It is best seen as a case of a family arrangement. Almost the only reported case in which an act of generosity having contractual force has been held to create a licence is *Foster* v *Robinson* [1951] 1 KB 149 where a tenant surrendered his statutory tenancy in return for a promise that he could live in his cottage rent free for the rest of his life.

5.6   Family arrangements

Instances of binding family arrangements have been given in 3.4 above. In each case, notwithstanding the fact that the occupier had possession, the court held that a licence had been created. However, it is likely that only in *Errington* v *Errington and Woods* (above) and *Hardwick* v *Johnson* [1978] 2 All ER 935 was exclusive possession really conferred upon the occupier. The other cases are cases where the owner of the property was a more or less frequent visitor, and accordingly may be sustainable on the ground that the occupier did not have exclusive possession (eg *Tanner* v *Tanner* [1975] 3 All ER 776; *Chandler* v *Kerley* [1978] 2 All ER 942).

However the mere fact that grantor and grantee are members of the same family does not of itself prevent a tenancy from being created. In *Collier* v *Hollinshead* (1984) 272 EG 941 an arrangement was entered into after the death of a farmer. The farmer's son wished to carry on farming the land, and he was allowed to do so by his mother (who was one of the executors). He paid for his occupation of the farm at a rate which was more than nominal, but less than the market rent. Scott J held that the parties intended to enter into legal relations, and that since the son had given consideration for the grant and had been given exclusive possession, a tenancy had been created.

5.7   Building agreements

It is common to find that where a person undertakes substantial building work in return for the grant of a leasehold interest in the site, the grant of the lease is postponed until satisfactory completion of the building work, and that during the building period the developer is expressed to be a licensee. Factually, it is likely that the developer would be found to have exclusive possession of the site. Prima facie therefore, the developer will be a tenant, and the building agreement treated as an agreement for lease. However, it may be that the court would hold that the transitional nature of the rights granted to the developer under a building agreement was a circumstance sufficiently special to negative the presumption that a tenancy had been created.

5.8 Timesharing

Timesharing has grown in the last few years. There are various methods of organising a timesharing scheme. It may be done by the grant of a lease to each timesharer for a discontinuous term, such as the first week in August in each of the twenty years following the date of the lease. Such a lease appears to be valid (*Cottage Holiday Associates Ltd* v *Commrs of Customs and Excise* [1983] 2 WLR 861). However, an alternative method is to grant each timesharer a series of licences to use the accommodation during the chosen period, the grant of the licence being commonly evidenced by a transferable certificate. Despite the fact that timeshare accommodation is furnished and equipped, and repaired and maintained by the operator, it is likely that each timesharer has exclusive possession of the accommodation during the period of the licence. Since the transaction may be carried out as well by a lease as by a licence, it is unlikely that the circumstances will be sufficient to negative the creation of a tenancy.

5.9 Franchising

Franchising arrangements take many forms. Frequently the owner of the business provides the premises in which the business is carried on, and supplies the franchisee with the products to be sold. The franchisee will be granted a licence to occupy the property, and will account to the owner of the business for a specified proportion of the profits (or turnover). It is suggested that the relation of a franchisor and franchisee is probably sufficiently special as to negative any intention to create a tenancy. In *Shell-Mex and BP Ltd* v *Manchester Garages Ltd* [1971] 1 All ER 841 Sachs LJ said:

On looking at the substance of the matter as a whole, it becomes apparant that the dominant objective of the contractual relationship between the parties was to further the promotion of the sale of the plaintiff's products on the site which they had selected, with the aid of the structures and equipment which they had provided and over which they were to exercise a right of control—including a right to deal with the layout and equipment from time to time.

These factors led directly to his conclusion that the arrangement was in truth a licence. Clearly, there is a striking resemblance between the relationship thus described and that between franchisor and franchisee.

6 What Is To Be Done?

6.1 After *Street* v *Mountford*

Two general lessons may be learned from *Street* v *Mountford*. First, a contractual arrangement giving exclusive possession to an occupier at a rent will be held to be a tenancy. Although Lord Templeman refers to special circumstances which may negative the intention to create a tenancy, most of them are, on analysis, cases where the parties did not enter into a contract at all, or where the arrangement did not confer exclusive possession on the occupier. Secondly, the court is likely to be more robust than heretofore in the detection of shams and avoidance schemes.

Accordingly, it is necessary to reappraise some of the transactions which are available to parties who do not wish a fully protected tenancy to be created.

6.2 Sharing agreements

Clearly it is no longer safe for a property owner to enter into 'sharing agreements' whereunder a group of persons known to each other are to live together in residential accommodation. However, where the sharers are not previously known to each other and where the agreements with the owner are made at different times, they may yet be upheld. Where, for example an educational establishment takes a house or flat to be shared by students, the students may well not become tenants (see eg *Groveside Properties Ltd* v *Westminster Medical School* (1983) 267 EG 678, where the educational establishment was held to be in occupation of the flat inhabited by students).

In addition, where the grantor actually intends himself to share the accommodation with the grantee, there can be no objection to the arrangement being recorded in writing. In such a case the sharer will not acquire exclusive possession and no tenancy will result.

6.3   Letting as multiple dwelling

A protected tenancy can only arise where a dwelling house is let as a separate dwelling (Rent Act 1977, s 1). This expression has been held to mean that the dwelling in question must be let as a single dwelling (*Horford Investments Ltd* v *Lambert* [1976] Ch 89). Thus where a house was let to an educational institution in order for that institution to accommodate students each of whom had the exclusive use of one room, the tenancy was held not to be protected (*St Catherine's College* v *Dorling* [1979] 1 All ER 250). In the case of an educational institution there is little danger of the occupiers themselves having protection (Rent Act 1977, s 8. However in other cases, although the head tenancy of the whole house may not be protected, the individual occupiers may now be held to be subtenants of their individual rooms. Where a group of persons intend to share a house or flat, each with the exclusive use of one room, it may be better for the tenancy to be granted to one of them alone, expressly for the purpose of multiple dwelling. That tenancy will not be protected. If the tenant in turn permits the other sharers to have the exclusive use of one room, then even if each sharer is held to be a tenant of that room, the likelihood is that the subtenancy would not be protected because:
  (i)   the subtenant will be sharing living accommodation with the tenant (*Baker* v *Turner* [1950] AC401; Rent Act 1977, s 21); and /or
  (ii) the tenant will be a resident landlord (Rent Act 1977, s 12).
However, caution must be exercised in view of the possible implications of *Street* v *Mountford* for *any* transaction (sham or not) which is designed to avoid Rent Act control (see 4.4 above).

6.4   Company lettings

A company to whom a dwelling is let is entitled to the benefit of rent control (*Carter* v *SU Carburettor Co* [1942] 2 KB 288) but not to security of tenure under the Rent Act 1977. It will only be entitled to security of tenure under Part II of the Landlord and Tenant Act 1954 in exceptional circumstances (*Chapman* v *Freeman* [1978] 3 All ER 878). Thus grew the practice of granting tenancies of dwellings to companies for the occupation of an officer or employee of the company, who was often named in the tenancy agreement. One such case was *Firstcross Ltd* v *East West (Export/Import) Ltd* (1980) 255 EG 355. On the termination of the tenancy the named occupier (who was a director of the company tenant) argued that he was entitled to a statutory tenancy on the ground that the company was the nominal tenant only, and he was the real tenant. The Court of Appeal rejected that argument. It does not appear from the report whether the director reimbursed the company with the amount of the rent. If he did, and if, as seems likely, he had the exclusive possession of the flat, it would now be arguable that he was a sub-tenant of the company. Although a sub-tenant does not acquire protection unless the subtenancy is lawful (Rent Act 1977, s 137) a landlord might find it difficult to argue that an arrangement which was contemplated by the terms of the company's own tenancy was unlawful. Moreover, in the light of the approach of the House of Lords to shams (in *Street* v *Mountford*) there is the added danger that a company letting of this kind will be categorised as a sham (see 4.4 above).

6.5   Eight month term

Where a landlord wishes to let for a term certain not exceeding eight months he may be able to avoid most of the effect of security of tenure by exploiting what is an apparent loophole in the Rent Act 1977. Under Case 13 of Schedule 15 to the Rent Act 1977 the court must make an order for possession where:

(i)   the dwelling house is let under a tenancy for a term of years certain not exceeding eight months (ie the tenancy cannot be brought to an end except by forfeiture);

(ii) before the start of the tenancy the landlord gave the tenant notice in writing that possession might be recovered under Case 13; and

(iii) the dwelling house was, at some time during the period of twelve months ending on the commencement of the tenancy, occupied under a right to occupy it for a holiday.

This case was designed to facilitate 'out of season' lettings in holiday resorts. However, the drafting is not limited to any particular type of property, nor does it require the landlord to prove that he has any particular intention with regard to the future of the property (eg to relet for holiday purposes). All that is required is that the property has been occupied for a holiday in the year preceding the fixed term letting, and the service of a notice on the tenant.

The term certain will be a protected tenancy, albeit that the landlord has a mandatory ground for possession. Accordingly, the tenant is entitled to the benefit of rent control (ie he may apply for the registration of a fair rent). Further, at the expiry of the term certain the tenant will become entitled to a statutory tenancy if he is then in occupation of the property as his residence. It follows, therefore, that Case 13 may be used even where it is envisaged that the tenancy will endure beyond eight months. All that is necessary is that the contractual term is limited to eight months or less.

6.6   Shorthold

The Housing Act 1980 introduced a new variety of protected tenancy called the shorthold tenancy. A shorthold tenancy is a tenancy granted for a term certain of not less than one year nor more than five years which satisfies the following conditions:

  (i)   it cannot be brought to an end by the landlord before the expiry of the term except in pursuance of a provision for forfeiture for non-payment of rent or breach of obligation;

 (ii)   before the grant the landlord has given the tenant notice in the prescribed form stating that the tenancy is to be a protected shorthold tenancy; and

(iii)   if the dwelling is in London, the rent does not exceed the registered rent (or an application for a registered rent is made during the first 28 days of the tenancy) (Housing Act 1980, s 52).

Where a dwelling house has been let on a protected shorthold tenancy and:

(i) there has been no grant of a further tenancy of the dwelling house (or if there has, the tenant was already in possession as protected or statutory tenant); and

(ii) possession proceedings are started within three months after the expiry of notice given to the tenant in the last three months of the term (or the three months preceding any anniversary of the term date)

then the court must make an order for possession (Rent Act 1977, Sched 15, Case 19). Shortholds have not proved popular (perhaps because of the political controversy which surrounded their introduction) but they may become more popular now that the trend towards the grant of licences has been halted.

6.7   Six month term

A tenancy of property occupied by the tenant for business purposes does not attract the protection of Part II of the Landlord and Tenant Act 1954 if it is granted for a term certain not exceeding six months unless:

(i) the tenancy contains provision for renewing the term or for extending it beyond six months from its beginning; or

(ii) the tenant has been in occupation for a period which, together with any period during which any predecessor in the carrying on of the business carried on by the tenant was in occupation, exceeds twelve months (Landlord and Tenant Act 1954, s 43(3)).

A term certain may contain a break clause (*Scholl Mfg Co Ltd* v *Clifton (Slim-Line) Ltd* [1967] Ch 41 at 51). It should be noted that when aggregating periods of business occupation, it is title to the business, not title to the property which is decisive. Thus where the owner of a business sells the business to a person to whom he grants a six month term, the landlord's own business occupation will be aggregated with the tenant's.

6.8   Contracting out: business tenancies

On the joint application of the intending landlord and tenant in relation to a tenancy for a term of years certain, the court may authorise an agreement excluding the operation of Part II of the Landlord and Tenant Act 1954 (Landlord and Tenant Act 1954, s 38(4)). A term of years certain includes a term for less than one year (*Re Land and Premises at Liss, Hants* [1971] Ch 986). As noted above, a term certain may contain a break clause. But it must be a term certain, and accordingly the court has no jurisdiction to authorise the 'contracting out' of a periodic tenancy, or a tenancy granted for a term certain and thereafter from year to year. Although s 38(4) appears to give the court a discretion whether or not to authorise the exclusion of the Act, in practice it invariably does. The practice was recognised by Lord Denning MR in *Hagee (London) Ltd* v *AB Erikson and Larson* [1976] QB 209:

We are told that the county court invariably approves such an agreement when it is made by business people properly advised by their lawyers. The court has no materials on which to refuse it.

Accordingly, where a landlord contemplates a short term arrangement (eg pending redevelopment) the safest course is to enter into a tenancy 'contracted out' of the Landlord and Tenant Act 1954.

Appendix

Form 1: Service agreement

Form 2: Licence for serviced accommodation

Form 3: Residential sharing agreement

Form 4: Shop within a shop

Form 5: Licence to share professional offices

Form 1: Service agreement

BY THIS AGREEMENT   of   ('the Employer')(1)
and   of   ('the Employee')(2)
AGREE as follows:

1. The Employer shall employ the Employee as caretaker of the Employer's property at
2. The duties of the Employee are:
    (i)   to act as caretaker of the property
    (ii) to clean the interior of the property three times each week
    (iii) to mow the lawns not less than six times each month during the growing season
    (iv) to prevent persons from trespassing on the property
3. For the better performance of their duties the Employee is required to live in the staff accommodation at the property as described in the Schedule
4. The Employer shall keep the staff accommodation in repair and shall pay (or indemnify the Employees against payment of) the general and water rates payable in respect of it
5. The Employee shall vacate the staff accommodation immediately upon termination (for whatever reason) of his employment
6. The Employee shall be remunerated at the rate of £   per week payable monthly in arrear (or such other amount as may be agreed from time to time)
7. In addition to the usual deductions the Employer shall be entitled to deduct the amount (if any) payable for gas and electricity consumed by the Employee in the staff accommodation
8. Either party may determine this agreement on two weeks' written notice, and the Employer may also determine it summarily if the Employee is seriously or deliberately in breach of his duty

Signed etc

Schedule

Form 2: Licence for serviced accommodation

BY THIS AGREEMENT   of ('the Owner')
  gives   of   ('the Occupier') licence
  to reside in Room No   at   ('the Building')
  on the following terms:

1. The Occupier shall pay £   per month for his occupation payable in advance on the first day of each month
2. The Occupier may use the communal washing and sanitary facilities in the Building and the communal kitchen television room and garden
3. The Occupier may only use the Room as his own residence and may not have any overnight guests or keep any pets
4. The Occupier must not cause any nuisance or annoyance to other residents in the Building
5. The Occupier must take reasonable care to prevent damage to the Room and its contents and must pay for any damage or breakages which he causes
6. The Occupier must not interfere with the Owner's rights of possession and control over the Room
7. The Owner will pay the general and water rates payable for the Building (including the Room if separately rated) and the television licence fee
8. The Owner will provide for the Occupier:
   - (i) one clean sheet one clean pillowcase and one clean towel every week
   - (ii) cleaning of the Room not less than twice a week and of the windows once a month
   - (iii) daily cleaning of the communal parts of the Building
   - (iv) hot water to the washing facilities and the kitchen in the Building and sanitary requisites
   - (v) a supply of gas to the kitchen
   - (vi) heating and lighting to the communal parts of the Building
   - (vii) a telephone for use by the Occupier in common with other residents (but the Occupier must pay for all his outgoing calls)
   - (viii) a refrigerator in the kitchen and a television for use by the Occupier in common with other residents
   - (ix) a gardener to keep the garden in good heart
   - (x) a caretaker to carry out such duties as the Owner may from time to time determine

(xi) all necessary household and table linen and crockery cutlery and cooking equipment

9. Personal belongings of the Occupier kept in the Room are kept there at the Occupier's own risk

10. This agreement may be terminated by four weeks' written notice given by either party

Signed etc

Form 3: Residential sharing agreement

BY THIS AGREEMENT   of   ('the Owner')(1)
and   of   ('the Sharer')(2)
AGREE as follows:

1. The Owner gives the Sharer personal permission to live in the property known as   ('the Property') and to use the furniture and other items listed in the Schedule in common with all other persons whom the Owner permits to live there
2. During the Sharer's period of residence at the Property he will pay the Owner £   per week payable in advance every Friday
3. The Sharer agrees with the Owner:
    (i) to keep the Property clean and tidy
    (ii) on leaving the Property to pay for the cleaning of all sheets blankets and other bedding used by the Sharer
    (iii) to pay for all damage and breakages caused by him
    (iv) to pay a fair proportion (to be determined by the Owner) of the cost of any gas and electricity consumed in the Property during the Sharer's period of residence and of the charges for the telephone (including equipment rental)
    (v) not to impede or obstruct the Owner's rights of possession and control over the Property
4. The Owner agrees with the Sharer:
    (i) not to permit more than   persons (including the Sharer) simultaneously to live in the Property
    (ii) in selecting persons to share the Property with the Sharer to consider his wishes and not to compel the Sharer to share a bedroom with a person of the opposite sex
    (iii) to remedy any item of disrepair of which the Sharer notifies the Owner
5. This agreement may be terminated by four weeks' written notice given by either party

Signed etc

Schedule

Form 4: Shop within a shop

AN AGREEMENT made the   of   198   between   of
('the Licensor')(1)
and   of   ('the Licensee')(2)
WHEREBY IT IS AGREED:

1.   The Licensor grants the Licensee licence to use Stall No   on
the   floor of the Licensor's store at   ('the
Store') together with the sanitary facilities and staff room during
such hours as the Licensor shall keep the Store open for trading.
2.   The Licensor shall:
(i) give the Licensee and his authorised staff access to the stall
through the Store during the opening hours
(ii) permit the Licensee at reasonable times outside the opening
hours to have access to the Stall for the purpose of restocking
it
(iii) be responsible for the security of the Licensee's goods outside
the opening hours
3.   The Licensee shall:
(i) pay the Licensor £   per week payable weekly in advance
every Friday
(ii) not impede or interfere with the Licensor's rights of
possession and control over the stall
(iii) not be entitled to a key to any entrance into the Store
(iv) sell and display for sale   and no other merchandise
(v) keep the stall and the aisles and passages surrounding it
clean and tidy and at least once a day place all refuse in
receptacles provided by the Licensor for that purpose
(vi) not do or permit to be done in the Store anything which in
the opinion of the Licensor may be detrimental to the
efficient and harmonious operation of the Store or its
reputation
(vii) comply with any written regulations made by the Licensor
to regulate activities carried on in the Store
3.   Either party may determine this agreement upon three months'
written notice and the Licensor may also determine it upon seven
days' written notice if the Licensee commits any breach of his
obligations

Signed etc

Form 5: Licence to share professional offices

BY THIS LICENCE which is made the   of   198
          of   ('the Licensor') grants to
          of   ('the Licensee') licence
to share with the Licensor the use of the Licensor's offices at
          ('the Offices') from   until
determined in accordance with the provisions of this licence

1.   The Licensee shall pay the Licensor £   a month on the first
     day of each month (the first payment to be made on signing)
2.   The Licensee shall be entitled:
     (i)   to carry on business as   in such part of the
           Offices (consisting of not less than one private office and
              square feet of other office space) as the Licensor shall
           from time to time direct
     (ii) to use (in common with the Licensor) the sanitary facilities
           in the Offices
     (iii) to instal a telephone line (and all necessary telephone
           receivers) for his own exclusive use
     (iv) to instal his own office furniture and equipment in the
           Offices
3.   The Licensee shall not:
     (i)   impede or interfere with the Licensor's rights of possession
            and control of the Offices
     (ii)   use the Offices for any purpose other than for the business
            mentioned in clause 2(i) above
     (iii) be entitled to a key to the Offices
     (iv)   do anything which may avoid or increase the premium
            payable for any policy of insurance maintained by the
            Licensor or to which he is liable to contribute
     (v)   alter the Offices or their internal layout
     (vi)   interfere with the conduct of the Licensor's business as a

     (vii) solicit or attempt to solicit any client of the Licensor
     (viii) read or make copies of any books (other than published
            works of reference) papers or documents addressed to or in
            the possession or custody of the Licensor
     (ix)   permit or suffer the doing of anything prohibited by this
            clause
4.   The Licensor shall:
     (i)   try his best to give the Licensee and his staff and clients
            access to the Offices during normal office hours

    (ii) pay the general and water rates payable for the Offices and the rent payable to the Licensor's landlord

   (iii) keep the sanitary facilities in working order and properly cleaned and equipped

   (iv) keep the Offices adequately heated and lit during normal office hours

    (v) indemnify the Licensee against any breach by the Licensor of any of the terms upon which the Licensor holds the Offices

5.   The Licensor shall not:

    (i) interfere with the conduct of the Licensee's business

   (ii) solicit or attempt to solicit any client of the Licensor

   (iii) read or make copies of any books (other than published works of reference) papers or documents addressed to or in the possession or custody of the Licensee

   (iv) permit or suffer the doing of anything prohibited by this clause

6.   Either party may terminate this agreement by three months' written notice and the Licensor may also terminate it by two weeks' written notice if the Licensee commits a serious breach of his obligations

Signed etc